APPLE WATCH SE 3
USER GUIDE

Step-by-Step Instructions for Setup, Navigation, Fitness, Health, Customization, and Everyday Productivity

Kieran B. Vossler

Apple Watch SE 3

USER GUIDE

Step-by-Step Instructions for Setup,
Navigation, Fitness, Health, Customization,
and Everyday Productivity

KIERAN B. VOSSLER

Copyright © 2025 Kieran B. Vossler

Disclaimer

This guide is an independent publication and is not affiliated with, authorized, sponsored, or endorsed by Apple Inc. "Apple," "Apple Watch," "watchOS," and other related trademarks are the property of Apple Inc. and are used here for identification purposes only.

The information in this book is provided for educational and reference purposes. While care has been taken to ensure accuracy, the author and publisher accept no liability for any errors, omissions, or results arising from its use.

Readers should always consult Apple's official documentation, instructions, and safety guidelines.

Table Of Contents

Introduction

Congratulations on your new **Apple Watch SE (3rd Generation)!** This smartwatch is more than just a timepiece, it's a powerful companion for health, fitness, productivity, and everyday convenience. Whether you want to track your workouts, monitor your health, stay connected on the go, or simplify daily tasks, your Apple Watch SE 3 can help.

By the end of this guide, you'll be able to **set up, navigate, customize, and use your watch confidently**, unlocking its full potential.

Keep your watch and iPhone nearby while exploring features, it makes pairing, syncing, and learning much faster.

What's New in the SE 3

The **Apple Watch SE (3rd Gen)** introduces several upgrades over previous models:

1. **S10 Chip:** Faster and more energy-efficient performance for smoother app usage and better battery life.
2. **Always-On Display:** Check the time, notifications, and watch faces without raising your wrist.
3. **5G Connectivity:** Enjoy faster data speeds and seamless streaming on supported cellular models.
4. **Enhanced Durability:** Improved water and dust resistance, plus a stronger display for active users.
5. **Advanced Health Features:** Sleep tracking, heart rate monitoring, temperature sensing, and fall detection.
6. **Faster Charging:** Spend less time plugged in and more time using your watch.

Even if you aren't a fitness enthusiast, exploring health features can help you **prevent issues and stay more aware of your daily habits.**

Who This Book Is For

This guide is designed for:

- **Beginners:** Step-by-step instructions make it easy to learn your watch, even if you're new to Apple devices.
- **Fitness Enthusiasts:** Track workouts, heart rate, and activity rings while learning tips for smarter training.
- **Productivity Seekers:** Use calendar, reminders, email, and shortcuts to simplify daily tasks and save time.

Think of this guide as your personal **Apple Watch trainer,** follow each chapter in order for the best results.

How to Use This Book

To get the most out of this guide:

1. **Follow Step-by-Step Instructions:** Each chapter provides detailed steps for setup, navigation, and feature use.

2. **Use Pro Tips:** Highlighted tips help you save time, avoid mistakes, and explore hidden functionalities.

3. **Refer to Appendices:** Quick reference guides, glossary terms, and comparisons help you troubleshoot and expand knowledge.

4. **Interactive Learning:** Try out each step on your watch as you read. Pausing to practice improves retention.

Keep your iPhone and Apple Watch nearby while reading, hands-on practice reinforces learning.

By completing this introduction, you should have a clear understanding of the **key upgrades of the SE 3**, know whether this guide is suited to your needs, and feel prepared to follow the step-by-step instructions in the coming chapters.

You now have the context and tools to start using your Apple Watch SE confidently and efficiently, setting the stage for hands-on learning, personalization, and maximizing productivity, fitness, and health tracking from day one.

Chapter One

Getting Started

Your Apple Watch SE (3rd Generation) is ready to help you track your health, stay connected, and boost productivity. This chapter will guide you step by step through unboxing, choosing the right case size, pairing it with your iPhone, and updating watchOS so you can start using your watch confidently.

Unboxing and Checking Contents

When you first open your Apple Watch SE (3rd Gen) box, ensure you have all the included items:

- **Apple Watch SE (3rd Gen)**
- **Watch Band(s):** Usually included in two sizes to fit different wrists
- **Magnetic Charging Cable**
- **USB Power Adapter** (depending on region)
- **Quick Start Guide and Warranty Information**

Step-by-Step Checklist:

1. Place all items on a flat surface.
2. Verify the watch face and back are free from scratches or defects.
3. Confirm the band is compatible with your preferred wrist size.
4. Keep the charging cable handy, you'll need it for initial setup and charging.

Pro Tip: Keep the packaging until you confirm the watch functions properly, in case you need to return or exchange it.

Case Sizes and Variants (40mm vs 44mm)

Apple Watch SE (3rd Gen) comes in **two case sizes**:

- **40mm Case:** Best suited for smaller wrists. Offers a slightly smaller display but full functionality.

- **44mm Case:** Better for larger wrists and easier readability of text and notifications.

Step-by-Step Guidance for Choosing Your Size:

1. Measure your wrist circumference using a tape measure.
   - Small/Medium wrists (approx. 130–200mm): 40mm recommended
   - Medium/Large wrists (approx. 150–220mm): 44mm recommended
2. Consider **visual preference**: a larger screen is easier to interact with, while a smaller case feels lighter.
3. Try the band sizes before finalizing your choice; the watch is adjustable but comfort is key.

Pro Tip: If you plan to use your watch for **workouts or outdoor activities**, a slightly larger case (44mm) can make reading metrics mid-exercise easier.

Initial Setup and Pairing with iPhone

Your Apple Watch needs to pair with an iPhone running the latest iOS version to unlock its full functionality.

Step-by-Step Setup:

1. **Power On Your Watch**
   - Press and hold the side button until the Apple logo appears.
2. **Bring Your iPhone Close**
   - Make sure Bluetooth is enabled on your iPhone.
   - A "Use Your iPhone to Set Up This Apple Watch" prompt will appear.
3. **Follow On-Screen Instructions on iPhone**
   - Tap **Continue** and align the watch face with the iPhone camera.
   - Wait for the watch to sync. This may take a few minutes.

4. **Sign In with Apple ID**
   - ○ Enter your Apple ID credentials to enable iCloud, Apple Pay, and other features.

5. **Set Up Preferences**
   - ○ Choose wrist (left or right), enable passcode, and customize activity tracking settings.

Pro Tip: Keep your watch near your iPhone during setup for faster syncing and fewer connectivity interruptions.

Updating watchOS

After pairing, always check for the **latest watchOS updates** to ensure your watch runs smoothly and has the latest features.

Step-by-Step Update Process:

1. On your **iPhone**, open the **Watch app**.
2. Tap **General > Software Update**.

3. If an update is available, tap **Download and Install**.

4. Keep your watch on its charger and connected to Wi-Fi.

5. Wait for the update to complete; the watch will restart automatically.

Pro Tip: Updates can take 20–40 minutes. Schedule updates when you don't need immediate use of your watch.

You now know how to **unbox, inspect, and prepare your Apple Watch SE**, understand the **differences between 40mm and 44mm cases**, successfully **pair it with your iPhone**, and **update watchOS** to the latest version.

With these foundational steps completed, your watch is fully prepared for use, and you're ready to move on to explore navigation, personalization, and productivity features in the following chapters.

Chapter Two

Navigation and Controls

Navigating your Apple Watch SE efficiently is the key to unlocking its full potential. This chapter will guide you through every aspect of navigation, including the Digital Crown, side button, touchscreen gestures, Control Center, Notification Center, and the Dock. By the end, you'll move seamlessly between apps, settings, and notifications.

Digital Crown and Side Button Functions

The **Digital Crown** and **side button** are the main physical controls of your Apple Watch SE, each with multiple functions:

Digital Crown Functions:

1. **Single Press:** Returns you to the watch face from any app or screen.
2. **Turn (Scroll/Zoom):**
   - Scroll through long lists (like notifications or contacts) without swiping.
   - Zoom in/out of maps or photos.
   - Adjust volume when playing music or media.
3. **Press and Hold:** Activate Siri for voice commands.
4. **Double-Press:** Switch between the two most recently used apps for quick multitasking.

Side Button Functions:

1. **Single Press:** Opens the Dock, which shows your most recently used or favorite apps.
2. **Press and Hold:** Access Emergency SOS, Power Off, and Medical ID.
3. **Double-Click:** Use Apple Pay for quick, contactless transactions.

Step-by-Step Example:

- To check your notifications quickly, press the Digital Crown to go to the watch face, then swipe down for Notification Center.
- To adjust music volume, open the Music app and turn the Digital Crown until the sound reaches your desired level

Pro Tip: Use the **Digital Crown instead of swiping** when scrolling through long lists, this prevents accidental taps and gives smoother control.

Touchscreen Gestures (Tap, Swipe, Press, etc.)

The touchscreen allows for quick, intuitive interaction with your watch:

1. **Tap:**
    - Select apps, open notifications, or confirm commands.
    - Single-tap buttons to activate features.

2. **Swipe Up:**
   - Opens the **Control Center**, giving quick access to settings like battery, airplane mode, and connectivity.

3. **Swipe Down:**
   - Opens the **Notification Center**, showing recent alerts, messages, and reminders.

4. **Swipe Left/Right:**
   - Change between watch faces.
   - Swipe through certain apps (like the Activity app) to access different views.

5. **Press and Hold (Haptic Touch):**
   - Customize watch faces.
   - Access secondary menus in apps (e.g., long-press a message to reply with emojis).

Step-by-Step Example:

- To customize a watch face, press and hold the current face, swipe left or right to select a new one, then tap **Edit**.
- To dismiss notifications quickly, swipe left on any alert and tap **Clear**.

Pro Tip: Practice these gestures slowly at first, accuracy improves with familiarity, and it prevents accidental app closures.

Control Center and Notification Center

Control Center: Provides quick access to essential settings:

1. Swipe **up from the bottom** of any watch face to open it.
2. Toggle settings such as Airplane Mode, Do Not Disturb, and Silent Mode.

3. Check battery percentage and enable Low Power Mode if needed.

4. Tap the **Walkie-Talkie icon** to start an instant conversation.

Notification Center: Keeps you up-to-date with alerts and messages:

1. Swipe **down from the top** of the watch face.

2. Scroll with the Digital Crown or your finger to see recent notifications.

3. Tap a notification to open it and take action (reply to a message, view an email, or dismiss an alert).

4. Swipe left on a notification to **clear it individually** or tap **Clear All** to remove all notifications.

Pro Tip: Customize which controls appear in the Control Center via the iPhone **Watch app > Control Center > Customize Controls**. Place your most-used options at the top for faster access.

App Switching and Dock

The Dock helps you **switch between apps quickly** without returning to the home screen:

1. **Open the Dock:** Press the side button once.
2. **Scroll Through Apps:** Use the Digital Crown or swipe up/down to browse.
3. **Select an App:** Tap the app icon to open it immediately.
4. **Close or Return:** Press the side button again to return to the watch face.

Step-by-Step Example:

- While checking your Activity app, press the side button to open the Dock, scroll to Music, tap it, and start playback, then return to the watch face by pressing the side button again.

Pro Tip: Use the Dock for your **most-used apps** to avoid searching for them each time. You can also pin your favorite apps in the Watch app on iPhone for faster access.

Mastering these navigation and control features ensures smoother multitasking, faster access to notifications and apps, and sets a solid foundation for personalizing your watch, managing productivity tools, and tracking fitness and health in the upcoming chapters.

Chapter Three

Watch Faces and Personalization

Your Apple Watch SE is highly customizable, allowing you to create a personalized experience that fits your style, productivity needs, and fitness goals. This chapter will guide you through **changing watch faces, adding and customizing widgets (called complications), organizing your watch face gallery, and using photos as watch faces** so your watch is both functional and visually appealing.

Changing Watch Faces

Watch faces allow you to **quickly access the information you need** while reflecting your personal style.

Step-by-Step to Change a Watch Face:

1. **Press and Hold the Current Watch Face**
   - Lightly press and hold your watch face until it zooms out and displays the current watch faces.

2. **Swipe Left or Right**
   - Scroll through pre-installed watch faces.

3. **Select a Face**
   - Tap on the desired face to activate it.

4. **Customize the Face** *(optional)*
   - Press and hold the face again, then tap **Edit**.
   - Swipe left or right to access different customization options such as colors, complications, or dial styles.

Pro Tip: Create **different faces for specific activities**, like one for workouts showing heart rate and Activity rings, and another for work with calendar and reminders.

Adding and Customizing Widgets (Complications)

Widgets, or **complications**, show information from apps directly on your watch face.

Step-by-Step to Add or Customize Complications:

1. **Enter Customization Mode**
   - Press and hold the watch face, then tap **Edit**.
2. **Select the Complications Layer**
   - Swipe to the complications section. Each watch face supports a different number and layout of complications.
3. **Add or Change a Complication**
   - Tap a complication spot.
   - Scroll through the available options using the Digital Crown.
   - Tap the desired complication to apply it.
4. **Save Your Changes**
   - Press the Digital Crown to exit customization mode.

Examples of Useful Complications:

- **Activity Rings:** Track movement, exercise, and standing goals.
- **Weather:** Quick glance at current conditions.
- **Heart Rate:** Monitor your heart during workouts.
- **Calendar:** See upcoming meetings or reminders.

Pro Tip: Use **complications strategically,** place your most-used apps in visible spots for quick access without opening the full app.

Organizing Your Watch Face Gallery

You can save and switch between multiple watch faces efficiently.

Step-by-Step to Organize Your Gallery:

1. **Open the Watch App on Your iPhone**
   - Go to the **Face Gallery** tab.
2. **Add a New Watch Face**
   - Scroll through faces and tap **Add** for any face you like.
3. **Reorder Faces**
   - Tap **Edit** to drag and reorder faces so the most-used ones appear first when swiping on your watch.
4. **Delete Unused Faces**
   - Swipe left on a face in the Watch app and tap **Remove** to declutter.

Pro Tip: Keep a **mix of work, leisure, and fitness faces** to match your daily routines and avoid clutter.

Using Photos as Watch Faces

You can use personal photos to create a watch face with memories or favorite images.

Step-by-Step to Set a Photo Face:

1. **Open the Photos App on Your Watch or iPhone**
   - Select the photo you want to use.
2. **Create the Watch Face**
   - Tap the **Share** icon on iPhone, then choose **Create Watch Face**.
   - Choose **Photos Watch Face** or **Kaleidoscope** style.
3. **Customize the Face**
   - Add complications if desired.
   - Tap **Add** to apply the face to your watch.
4. **Switch to Your Photo Face**
   - Press and hold the watch face, swipe to your new photo face, and tap to activate.

Pro Tip: Use multiple photo faces for different moods or events, this can make your watch feel fresh and personalized every day.

By mastering watch face personalization, your Apple Watch SE becomes both a functional tool and a stylish accessory, reflecting your lifestyle, priorities, and personal taste. With these skills, switching between work, fitness, and leisure modes becomes seamless, improving both efficiency and enjoyment of your watch.

Chapter Four

Communication Features

Your Apple Watch SE allows you to stay connected without constantly checking your iPhone. This chapter covers **calls, messages, email, using Siri effectively, and Walkie-Talkie mode**, helping you communicate efficiently while on the go.

Calls, Messages, and Email

Your Apple Watch SE makes it easy to manage calls, text messages, and emails directly from your wrist.

Making and Receiving Calls:

1. **Make a Call:**
   - Open the **Phone app** on your watch.
   - Tap **Contacts** or **Keypad** to dial a number.
   - Tap the **call icon** to initiate the call.

2. **Receive a Call:**
   - When a call comes in, tap the **green button** to answer or **red button** to decline.
   - Swipe up to **send a quick message** instead of answering.

Sending Messages:

1. Open the **Messages app** on your watch.
2. Tap **New Message** or select an existing conversation.
3. **Use one of three methods to send a message:**
   - **Dictation:** Speak your message and it will convert to text.
   - **Emoji:** Select an emoji from the list.
   - **Preset Replies:** Tap from a list of quick responses.

Managing Email:

1. Open the **Mail app** on your watch.
2. Scroll using the **Digital Crown** to read new messages.

3. Tap a message to read, reply with dictation or preset replies, or mark it as read/unread.

Pro Tip: Keep your **messages concise** when using dictation, especially in noisy environments, for better accuracy.

Using Siri Effectively

Siri is your voice assistant on the Apple Watch SE, capable of sending messages, starting workouts, setting reminders, and more.

Step-by-Step to Use Siri:

1. **Activate Siri:**
   - Press and hold the **Digital Crown**, or
   - Raise your wrist and say, "**Hey Siri**."
2. **Speak Your Command:**
   - Examples: "Send a message to John," "Start a 30-minute run," "Set a reminder for 3 PM."

3. **View Siri Responses:**

    ○ Siri will display the response on-screen and, if appropriate, speak it aloud.

Tips for Accurate Siri Use:

- Speak clearly and at a moderate pace.
- Use specific commands to get precise results.
- Ensure your watch has a stable internet connection for best performance.

Pro Tip: You can **combine dictation with Siri** for sending messages hands-free while walking or exercising.

Walkie-Talkie Mode

Walkie-Talkie allows instant push-to-talk conversations with other Apple Watch users.

Step-by-Step Setup and Use:

1. Open the **Walkie-Talkie app** on your watch.
2. Tap **Add Friends** and select a contact who also has an Apple Watch.

3. Wait for them to accept your invitation.

4. **Send a Message:**
   ○ Tap a friend's name, hold the talk button, speak, then release to send.

5. **Receive Messages:**
   ○ You'll get an alert, then tap to listen and respond immediately.

Pro Tip: Use Walkie-Talkie in **quiet spaces or with headphones** for clear audio, and turn off notifications in noisy environments to avoid disruption.

You should now be able to **make and receive calls, send messages and emails, use Siri efficiently, and communicate instantly with Walkie-Talkie mode**. Mastering these features allows you to stay connected, hands-free when needed, and respond quickly to messages and calls, making your Apple Watch SE a powerful tool for personal and professional communication, whether at work, exercising, or on the move.

Chapter Five

Health and Fitness Tracking

Your Apple Watch SE is a powerful tool for monitoring your health and keeping you active. This chapter will guide you through **heart rate monitoring, sleep tracking, understanding activity rings, and using the Workout app**, helping you maintain a healthier lifestyle and meet your fitness goals.

Heart Rate Monitoring

The Apple Watch SE continuously tracks your heart rate and provides real-time insights.

Step-by-Step to Monitor Your Heart Rate:

1. **Open the Heart Rate App** on your watch.
2. **View Your Current Heart Rate:** The app displays your heart rate in beats per minute (BPM).

3. **Check Resting and Walking Heart Rate:**
   Scroll down in the app to see your average resting and walking heart rate.
4. **Set Notifications for High or Low Heart Rate:**
   - Open the Watch app on your iPhone > Heart > High Heart Rate and Low Heart Rate.
   - Set thresholds for alerts when your heart rate goes above or below these levels.

Pro Tip: Use **Heart Rate notifications** to detect unusual patterns early, this can help you take timely action and consult a healthcare professional if needed.

Sleep Score and Tracking

Tracking sleep helps you understand your rest patterns and improve overall health.

Step-by-Step to Track Sleep:

1. **Set Up Sleep in the Health App on iPhone:**
   - Open **Health app > Sleep > Full Schedule & Options**.
   - Set your **bedtime, wake-up time, and sleep goal**.

2. **Wear Your Watch Overnight:**
   - Ensure the watch has at least 30% battery before bed, or place it on the charger while setting up a charge schedule.

3. **View Sleep Data:**
   - Open the **Sleep app** on the watch or the **Health app** on your iPhone.
   - Review your **sleep stages, total sleep time, and sleep trends** over days or weeks.

Pro Tip: Enable **Wind Down mode** to reduce distractions before sleep, and wear your watch snugly for accurate tracking.

Activity Rings Explained

The three Activity Rings help you track daily movement and exercise goals:

1. **Move Ring (Red):** Tracks active calories burned throughout the day.
2. **Exercise Ring (Green):** Tracks minutes of brisk activity or workouts.
3. **Stand Ring (Blue):** Encourages standing at least one minute per hour for 12 hours daily.

Step-by-Step to Use Rings Effectively:

1. Open the **Activity app** to see your current progress.
2. Tap each ring for more detailed insights.
3. Set **personalized goals** in the Watch app > Activity.
4. Use **stand reminders and notifications** to close your rings consistently.

Pro Tip: Set reminders to **stand and move** to ensure your blue ring closes each day, this supports cardiovascular health and reduces sedentary behavior.

Using the Workout App

The Workout app tracks specific exercises and gives detailed metrics for each session.

Step-by-Step to Start a Workout:

1. Open the **Workout app** on your watch.
2. Scroll through workout types (running, cycling, swimming, yoga, etc.).
3. Tap your chosen workout.
4. Press **Start** and begin exercising.

During the Workout:

- Swipe to see metrics like **heart rate, calories, pace, distance, and time**.
- Use the **Digital Crown** to adjust music volume if playing audio.

Ending the Workout:

1. Swipe right and tap **End**.
2. Review your **summary**, including total calories, average heart rate, and duration.
3. Sync automatically to the **Health app** on your iPhone for long-term tracking.

Pro Tip: Use **customized workout goals** to challenge yourself and monitor progress over time.

You should now be able to **monitor your heart rate, track your sleep, understand and close your activity rings, and start and manage workouts** effectively.

Mastering these health and fitness tools allows you to stay active, improve sleep quality, and gain valuable insights into your overall well-being, making your Apple Watch SE an essential companion for a healthier, more active lifestyle.

Chapter Six

Advanced Health and Safety

The Apple Watch SE offers **advanced features that go beyond basic health tracking**, helping you monitor critical health metrics and stay safe in emergencies. This chapter covers **sleep apnea detection, temperature tracking, Emergency SOS, fall detection, and Medical ID setup**, providing step-by-step guidance so you can make the most of these powerful tools.

Sleep Apnea Detection and Temperature Tracking

Monitoring sleep and body temperature can provide early insights into potential health issues, such as sleep apnea or abnormal temperature trends.

Step-by-Step for Sleep Apnea Detection:

1. **Enable Sleep Tracking:**
   - On your iPhone, open the **Health app >
     Sleep > Full Schedule & Options**.
   - Turn on **Track Sleep with Apple Watch**.

2. **Wear the Watch Overnight:**
   - Ensure the watch is snug but comfortable
     on your wrist.
   - Charge the watch before bed to ensure it
     lasts through the night.

3. **Review Your Sleep Metrics:**
   - Open the **Health app > Sleep** the next
     morning.
   - Check **sleep stages, respiratory rate,
     heart rate during sleep**, and any
     irregularities.
   - Trends over multiple nights can indicate
     potential sleep apnea or disruptions in
     breathing.

Step-by-Step for Temperature Tracking:

1. Open the **Health app** > **Body Measurements** > **Temperature**.
2. Wear your watch consistently at night for accurate readings.
3. Review trends in your overnight **body or skin temperature**, which may reflect illness, infection, or hormonal changes.

Pro Tip: Use **consistent bedtimes and proper watch placement** to get the most reliable sleep and temperature data. Compare trends over weeks, not just a single night, for actionable insights.

Emergency SOS and Fall Detection

The Apple Watch SE can **automatically call for help and alert your emergency contacts** if you experience a serious fall or health emergency.

Emergency SOS Setup and Use:

1. **Activate SOS in an Emergency:**
   - Press and hold the **side button** until the **Emergency SOS slider** appears.
   - Drag the slider to call local emergency services, or continue holding the button to automatically call without sliding.

2. **Automatic Notifications:**
   - After triggering SOS, the watch sends your location to your **emergency contacts** automatically.
   - Contacts receive a message with your location and can track it until help arrives.

Fall Detection Setup and Use:

1. Open the **Watch app on your iPhone > Emergency SOS > Fall Detection**.
2. Choose **Always On** (for general use) or **Only During Workouts** (to reduce false alerts during daily activities).

3. **How It Works:**

   - If a hard fall is detected, your watch vibrates, sounds an alert, and displays an option to contact emergency services.
   - If you do not respond within **60 seconds**, the watch automatically calls emergency services and alerts your emergency contacts with your location.

Pro Tip: Enable fall detection **especially during workouts or outdoor activities** to maximize safety, and make sure your watch is snug but comfortable to prevent accidental false alarms.

Medical ID Setup

Medical ID provides **first responders with critical health information** even when your phone or watch is locked.

Step-by-Step to Set Up Medical ID:

1. Open the **Health app** > **Medical ID** > **Edit**.
2. Fill in all relevant information:
   - Name, date of birth, blood type, medical conditions, allergies, and medications.
   - Add **emergency contacts** with their phone numbers.
   - Select a preferred language for communication.
3. **Enable "Show When Locked"** so that anyone can access this critical information from your watch or iPhone in an emergency without unlocking the device.
4. **Save Changes:** Tap **Done** to store your Medical ID securely.

Pro Tip: Regularly **update your Medical ID** if medications, health conditions, or emergency contacts change. This ensures first responders have the most accurate information.

By fully utilizing these features, your Apple Watch SE becomes not only a tool for daily fitness and wellness but also a **critical safety device**.

Proper setup ensures you are prepared for emergencies, can alert help when needed, and provide essential health information to first responders, offering peace of mind during workouts, travel, or unexpected health events.

Chapter Seven

Apps and Productivity

Your Apple Watch SE is not just a fitness tracker, it's a **powerful productivity and lifestyle companion**. With the right setup, it can help you stay organized, communicate efficiently, navigate, and handle financial transactions, all from your wrist. This chapter covers **installing and managing apps, using Calendar, Reminders, Notes, and Maps, and setting up Apple Pay and Wallet**, with step-by-step guidance and practical tips for everyday use.

Installing and Managing Apps

Apple Watch apps extend your watch's functionality, from productivity tools to entertainment, fitness, and lifestyle apps.

Step-by-Step to Install Apps:

1. **Open the App Store:**
   - On your Apple Watch: Press the Digital Crown > tap **App Store**.
   - On your iPhone: Open the **Watch app > App Store** tab.

2. **Browse or Search:**
   - Scroll through featured apps, categories, or search for a specific app using dictation or keyboard.

3. **Download the App:**
   - Tap **Get** or the app's price to download.
   - Authenticate using your Apple ID, Face ID, or Touch ID as prompted.

4. **Wait for Installation:**
   - Apps will appear on your watch's Home Screen (grid view) or Dock once installed.

Managing Apps on Your Watch:

1. **Rearranging Apps:**
   - Press and hold any app icon until all icons jiggle.
   - Drag the app to your preferred position.
   - Press the Digital Crown to save changes.

2. **Deleting Apps:**
   - Press and hold the app icon until it jiggles.
   - Tap the **X icon** or **Remove App**.
   - Confirm deletion.

3. **Dock Management:**
   - Press the **side button** to open Dock.
   - Tap **Edit** on your iPhone Watch app to add favorite apps for quick access.

Practical Example: Install a **weather app** and add it as a complication on your watch face. This allows quick access without opening the app, keeping you informed during meetings or workouts.

Pro Tip: Use apps that **integrate with complications** to display important information, like upcoming calendar events or fitness metrics, directly on your watch face for quick glances.

Calendar, Reminders, Notes, and Maps

Your Apple Watch SE can act as a **personal assistant**, keeping you organized and on time.

Calendar:

1. Open the **Calendar app** on your watch.
2. Scroll using the **Digital Crown** to see daily, weekly, or monthly events.
3. Tap an event to view **details**, including location and invitees.
4. Add events using **Siri**: "Hey Siri, schedule a meeting at 10 AM tomorrow."

Reminders:

1. Open the **Reminders app**.

2. Tap **New Reminder** or use Siri to create one.

3. Set **time-based or location-based reminders**.

4. Mark reminders as complete by tapping the circle next to them.

Notes:

1. Open the **Notes app** synced from iPhone via iCloud.

2. Tap a note to read or edit using **dictation, Scribble, or emoji**.

3. Notes automatically sync across all devices connected to the same Apple ID.

Maps:

1. Open the **Maps app** on your watch.

2. Use Siri or tap **Search** to enter a destination.

3. Follow **turn-by-turn directions** displayed on your watch.

4. Haptic alerts gently tap your wrist when it's time to turn, no need to constantly look at the screen.

Practical Example: Use Maps to navigate to a nearby coffee shop while walking, receiving haptic cues for each turn, while Notes keeps your shopping list visible for reference.

Pro Tip: Combine **Calendar and Reminders** with Maps to receive location-based alerts, such as "Leave now for your meeting," so you arrive on time.

Apple Pay and Wallet Setup

Apple Pay makes **secure, contactless payments** fast and easy, eliminating the need to carry cards or cash.

Step-by-Step Setup:

1. Open the **Wallet app** on your watch or iPhone.
2. Tap **Add Card** > **Credit/Debit Card**.
3. Enter card details manually or scan your card with your iPhone camera.

4. Verify with your bank using **text message, app, or call**.

5. Once verified, your card is ready to use.

Using Apple Pay:

1. Double-click the **side button** to open Apple Pay.
2. Hold your watch near the contactless payment terminal.
3. Wait for the checkmark and gentle vibration confirming a successful payment.

Practical Example: Pay for a coffee during your morning run without taking your wallet or phone out of your pocket.

Pro Tip: Apple Pay is ideal for **quick transactions on the go**, especially during commuting, workouts, or grocery shopping. Set up multiple cards for convenience and flexibility.

You can now **install and manage apps**, efficiently use **Calendar, Reminders, Notes, and Maps**, and **set up and operate Apple Pay**.

Mastering these features turns your Apple Watch SE into a **central hub for productivity**, allowing you to manage tasks, navigate, and make payments effortlessly. With these tools, your watch helps streamline daily routines, save time, and keep your personal and professional life organized—without reaching for your iPhone.

Chapter Eight

Media and Entertainment

Your Apple Watch SE can serve as a **powerful media hub**, letting you enjoy music, podcasts, and audiobooks, pair with wireless earbuds, and even control smart home devices or Apple TV, all from your wrist. This chapter provides detailed instructions on **listening to media, connecting devices, and controlling entertainment systems**, maximizing your enjoyment and convenience.

Music, Podcasts, and Audiobooks

The Apple Watch SE lets you **listen to music, podcasts, and audiobooks offline or via streaming**, giving you entertainment on the go without needing your iPhone nearby.

Step-by-Step to Play Music:

1. Open the **Music app** on your watch.
2. Browse options:
   - **Library:** Music synced from your iPhone.
   - **Apple Music:** Stream tracks if connected to Wi-Fi or cellular.
3. Tap a playlist, album, or song to play.
4. Adjust volume using the **Digital Crown**.
5. Swipe left/right to skip tracks or pause/play.

Step-by-Step for Podcasts:

1. Open the **Podcasts app**.
2. Browse episodes by subscription, category, or downloaded shows.
3. Tap an episode to start playing.
4. Use **playback controls** to pause, skip, or rewind.

Step-by-Step for Audiobooks:

1. Open the **Books app** (Audiobooks section).
2. Tap an audiobook to resume playback or start a new one.
3. Adjust playback speed if needed.
4. Sync audiobooks from your iPhone or download for offline listening.

Pro Tip: Download playlists and podcasts offline before workouts or travel to avoid interruptions in areas with poor connectivity.

Pairing with Bluetooth Earbuds

Pairing your wireless headphones or earbuds with your Apple Watch SE provides **freedom to listen without carrying your iPhone**.

Step-by-Step to Pair Bluetooth Devices:

1. Put your earbuds into **pairing mode** (check manufacturer instructions).
2. Open **Settings > Bluetooth** on your watch.
3. Wait for the earbuds to appear under **Other Devices**.
4. Tap the device name to connect.
5. Once connected, audio will automatically route to your earbuds.

Pro Tip: Pair your earbuds in **advance of workouts or commutes** to save time and avoid connectivity delays. You can also manage multiple paired devices and switch between them quickly.

Controlling Home Devices and Apple TV

The Apple Watch SE can act as a **remote control for HomeKit-enabled devices and Apple TV**, allowing you to manage your environment without touching your phone or TV remote.

Step-by-Step to Control Home Devices:

1. Open the **Home app** on your watch.
2. Browse your HomeKit accessories: lights, thermostats, locks, etc.
3. Tap a device to turn it on/off, adjust brightness, or control settings.
4. Create **scenes** (e.g., "Movie Night") that adjust multiple devices at once.

Step-by-Step to Control Apple TV:

1. Open the **Remote app** on your watch.
2. Tap your Apple TV from the list of devices.
3. Use the **touchpad interface** to navigate menus, play/pause content, and adjust volume.
4. Use **Siri** to search or play specific shows: "Hey Siri, play *Stranger Things* on Apple TV."

Pro Tip: Set up **favorite HomeKit scenes** for quick access on your watch, like turning off all lights when leaving home or dimming lights for a movie night.

You should now be able to **stream or play music, podcasts, and audiobooks**, pair and manage Bluetooth earbuds, and **control smart home devices and Apple TV** from your wrist.

By mastering these media and entertainment features, your Apple Watch SE becomes a **central hub for audio and home entertainment**, allowing seamless listening, easy access to content, and convenient control of your smart home environment, perfect for workouts, commuting, or relaxing at home.

Chapter Nine

Connectivity and Battery Management

Your Apple Watch SE is only as powerful as its **connectivity and battery management**. With proper setup, you can stay connected to Wi-Fi, Bluetooth, cellular networks, and even manage family accounts. Additionally, understanding battery optimization and fast charging ensures your watch is ready when you need it. This chapter covers **network setup, Family Setup, battery maintenance, and charging strategies**.

Wi-Fi, Bluetooth, Cellular and 5G Setup

Proper network setup ensures your Apple Watch stays connected even when your iPhone is not nearby.

Step-by-Step for Wi-Fi Setup:

1. Open **Settings** > **Wi-Fi** on your watch.
2. Tap the network you want to join.
3. Enter the password using the watch keyboard or Scribble feature.
4. Once connected, a Wi-Fi icon appears in the Control Center.

Step-by-Step for Bluetooth Setup:

1. Open **Settings** > **Bluetooth** on your watch.
2. Put the device you want to pair (earbuds, headphones, or speakers) in **pairing mode**.
3. Tap the device name when it appears under **Other Devices** to connect.
4. Confirm the connection with a prompt if necessary.

Step-by-Step for Cellular & 5G Setup:

1. Open **Settings > Cellular > Set Up Cellular** on your watch.
2. Follow the prompts to connect your watch to your carrier.
3. Confirm your Apple Watch plan and activate cellular services.
4. Once active, the **cellular icon** appears on your watch face.

Pro Tip: Use **Wi-Fi for streaming media or software updates** to save cellular data, and enable **5G only when needed** for optimal battery life.

Family Setup

Family Setup allows you to **manage Apple Watches for family members**, especially kids or older adults, from your iPhone.

Step-by-Step for Family Setup:

1. Open the **Watch app on your iPhone > All Watches > Add Watch > Set Up for a Family Member**.
2. Follow prompts to **pair the watch** and create an Apple ID for the family member if needed.
3. Configure **cellular, location, and health settings** for safety and connectivity.
4. Enable **communication limits, Schooltime, and Activity goals** to manage usage.

Practical Example: Set up a child's Apple Watch with **limited communication and GPS tracking**, while allowing them to call emergency contacts.

Pro Tip: Family Setup is ideal for monitoring **health, location, and connectivity** for children or older adults who don't have an iPhone.

Battery Optimization and Fast Charging

Maintaining battery health ensures your watch lasts throughout the day and night.

Step-by-Step for Battery Optimization:

1. Open **Settings** > **Battery** on your watch to view usage and battery percentage.
2. Enable **Low Power Mode** when necessary (Settings > Battery > Power Reserve).
3. Limit background app refresh: Watch app on iPhone > General > Background App Refresh.
4. Reduce **screen brightness**: Settings > Display & Brightness > adjust brightness.

Step-by-Step for Fast Charging:

1. Use the **Apple Watch magnetic charger** and a compatible USB-C power adapter.
2. Place the watch on the charger with alignment magnets.

3. A **lightning bolt icon** indicates charging is in progress.

4. Fast charging can deliver a **50% charge in about 30 minutes**.

Pro Tip: A **15-minute charge before bed** ensures your watch has enough power to track sleep and overnight health metrics without interruptions.

Setting up Wi-Fi, Bluetooth, cellular, and 5G, manage **Family Setup accounts**, and implement **battery optimization and fast charging strategies** is now a possibility.

Mastering these connectivity and power features ensures your Apple Watch SE is always ready for use, keeps you connected to family and essential apps, and reliably tracks health and fitness, even during overnight wear or long days away from your iPhone.

Chapter Ten

Troubleshooting and Maintenance

Even the most advanced devices may experience minor issues over time. Proper maintenance and knowing how to troubleshoot can **extend your Apple Watch SE's lifespan and ensure smooth performance**. This chapter covers **common issues and fixes, resetting your watch, cleaning and care, and when to contact Apple Support**.

Common Issues and Fixes

Apple Watch SE may occasionally experience minor problems such as connectivity issues, app crashes, or display unresponsiveness.

Step-by-Step Troubleshooting:

1. **Watch Not Responding:**
   o Press and hold the **side button and Digital Crown simultaneously** for 10–15 seconds until the Apple logo appears.
   o This forces a **restart without erasing your data**.

2. **Apps Not Opening or Crashing:**
   o Close the app by pressing the **side button** > open Dock > swipe left on the app > tap **X** to close.
   o Reopen the app.
   o If the issue persists, **update the app** via the App Store or **restart the watch**.

3. **Connectivity Issues (Wi-Fi, Bluetooth, Cellular):**
   o Toggle **Airplane Mode** on and off in the Control Center.
   o Check paired devices in **Settings > Bluetooth**.
   o Restart both the watch and iPhone if the issue persists.

4. **Battery Draining Quickly:**
   - ○ Check **Battery settings** for apps consuming high power.
   - ○ Reduce screen brightness or disable **always-on display**.
   - ○ Ensure **background app refresh** is optimized.

Pro Tip: Restart your watch **regularly once or twice a week** to maintain smooth performance and prevent minor glitches.

Resetting Your Watch

Resetting can resolve persistent software issues or prepare the watch for a new user.

Step-by-Step to Reset Your Apple Watch:

1. **Back Up Your Watch:**
   - ○ Your watch automatically backs up to your iPhone. Ensure your iPhone is nearby and synced.

2. **Reset via Watch Settings:**

   ○ Open **Settings > General > Reset > Erase All Content and Settings**.

   ○ Enter your **passcode** if prompted.

   ○ Confirm to erase the watch.

3. **Reset via iPhone:**

   ○ Open the **Watch app > General > Reset > Erase Apple Watch Content and Settings**.

   ○ Follow on-screen prompts.

Practical Example: Resetting is useful before selling or gifting your watch to ensure all personal data is securely removed.

Cleaning and Caring for Your Apple Watch

Proper cleaning maintains the watch's appearance and functionality.

Step-by-Step Cleaning:

1. **Turn Off the Watch:** Press and hold the **side button > Power Off.**
2. **Remove Bands:** Detach leather, metal, or silicone bands for separate cleaning.
3. **Wipe the Watch Case:**
   - Use a **lint-free, slightly damp cloth.**
   - Avoid getting moisture in openings such as the microphone, speaker, or Digital Crown.
4. **Clean Bands:**
   - Silicone: Wash with **mild soap and water.**
   - Leather: Wipe with a **dry, soft cloth.**
   - Metal: Use a **damp cloth** and dry immediately.

5. **Dry Completely:** Allow the watch and bands to air-dry fully before reattaching or charging.

Pro Tip: Avoid harsh chemicals, abrasive materials, or high-pressure water to prevent damage. Regular cleaning **prevents dirt buildup** that can interfere with sensors.

When to Contact Apple Support

If issues persist after troubleshooting and resetting, contact Apple Support for professional assistance.

Situations Requiring Support:

- Watch does not turn on after multiple restarts.
- Persistent battery drain or charging issues.
- Faulty sensors (heart rate, ECG, or GPS) not responding.
- Hardware damage, such as cracked screen or water damage beyond rated limits.

Step-by-Step to Contact Apple Support:

1. Open the **Apple Support app** on your iPhone or visit **support.apple.com**.
2. Select **Apple Watch > Issues > Contact Support**.
3. Choose **chat, call, or schedule an appointment** at an Apple Store or Authorized Service Provider.

Pro Tip: Keep your **Apple ID and device serial number** handy when contacting support to expedite assistance.

After completing this chapter, you should be able to **identify and fix common issues, reset your watch when necessary, clean and maintain your Apple Watch SE, and recognize when professional support is needed.**

Regular maintenance and timely troubleshooting ensure your device **remains reliable, accurate, and safe to use**, while proper cleaning and care extend its lifespan and preserve performance. By mastering these skills, your Apple Watch SE stays in optimal condition, ready to support your fitness, productivity, and everyday needs.

Appendix A

Quick Reference Guide (Buttons, Gestures, Shortcuts)

Feature	Action / Gesture	Function
Digital Crown	Press once	Return to watch face
	Press and hold	Activate Siri
	Rotate	Scroll, zoom, or adjust settings
Side Button	Press once	Open Dock
	Press and hold	Access Emergency SOS

Touchscreen Gestures	Tap	Select or open apps
	Swipe left/right/up/down	Navigate between screens
	Force Touch (press firmly)	Access contextual menus / options
Shortcuts	Double-click Side Button	Apple Pay / Wallet
	Swipe up	Open Control Center
	Swipe down	Open Notification Center

Memorizing these gestures and shortcuts can save **time and make navigation more efficient**.

Appendix B

Glossary of Terms

- **Activity Rings:** Visual representation of your daily movement, exercise, and standing goals.
- **Complication:** Small widgets that display app information on your watch face.
- **Dock:** Quick-access menu for your favorite or recently used apps.
- **Family Setup:** Feature that allows managing Apple Watches for family members from your iPhone.
- **Haptic Feedback:** Gentle vibrations from the watch used for alerts or notifications.
- **Siri:** Apple's voice assistant for commands, reminders, navigation, and more.

Appendix C

Software Update and Support Policy

- Apple Watch SE receives **regular watchOS updates** that improve performance, add features, and enhance security.
- Updates are delivered via the **Watch app on your iPhone > General > Software Update**.
- Support is available via **Apple Support app, online resources, or Authorized Service Providers**.
- Always **backup your watch to your iPhone** before performing major updates.

Pro Tip: Keep your watch charged and connected to Wi-Fi during updates to avoid interruptions.

Appendix D

Comparison: Apple Watch SE vs Series 11 vs Ultra 3

Feature	Apple Watch SE (3rd Gen)	Series 11	Ultra 3
Chip	S10	S11	S11+
Display	Retina, Always-On	Retina, Always-On	Larger Always-On, Brighter
Connectivity	Wi-Fi, Bluetooth, Cellular	Wi-Fi, Bluetooth, 5G	Wi-Fi, Bluetooth, 5G
Durability	Water Resistant	Water Resistant	Extreme Durability, Higher Water Resistance

Health Sensors	Heart Rate, Sleep, Temp	ECG, Blood Oxygen	Advanced Sensors, ECG, Blood Oxygen, Temperature
Battery Life	~18 hrs	~18–20 hrs	~36 hrs, Fast Charge
Target Users	Everyday, Fitness	Advanced Health, Everyday	Adventure, Outdoor, Fitness Enthusiasts

Appendix E

Resources and Further Reading

- **Apple Official Website:** Search Online
- **Apple Support:** Search Online
- **Apple User Guides:** Search Online
- **Forums and Communities:** Apple Discussions, Reddit Apple Watch Communities
- **Books and Guides:** Fitness tracking guides, watchOS deep-dive manuals

Regularly check Apple's official site for **software updates, new features, and security advisories** to keep your watch running optimally.

Printed in Dunstable, United Kingdom